Ren

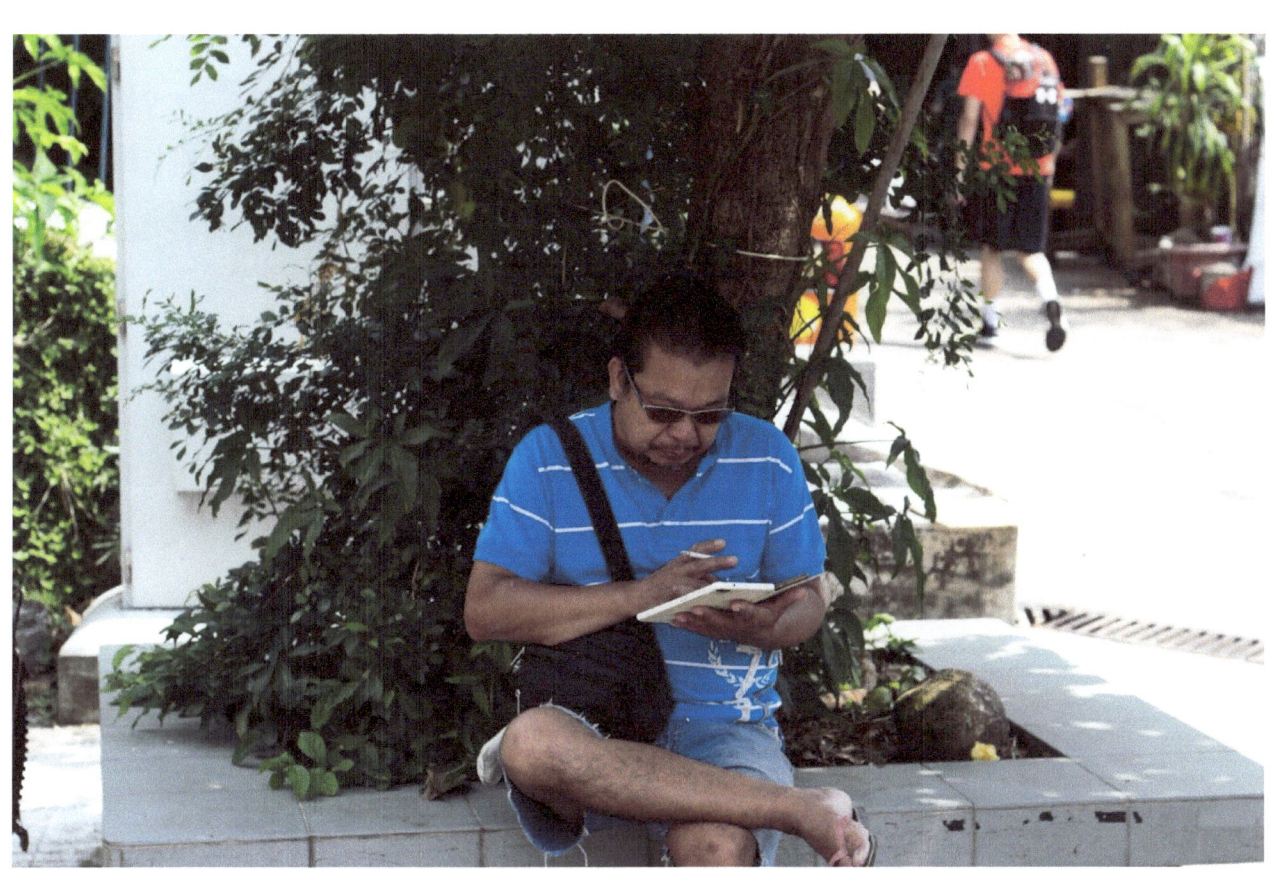

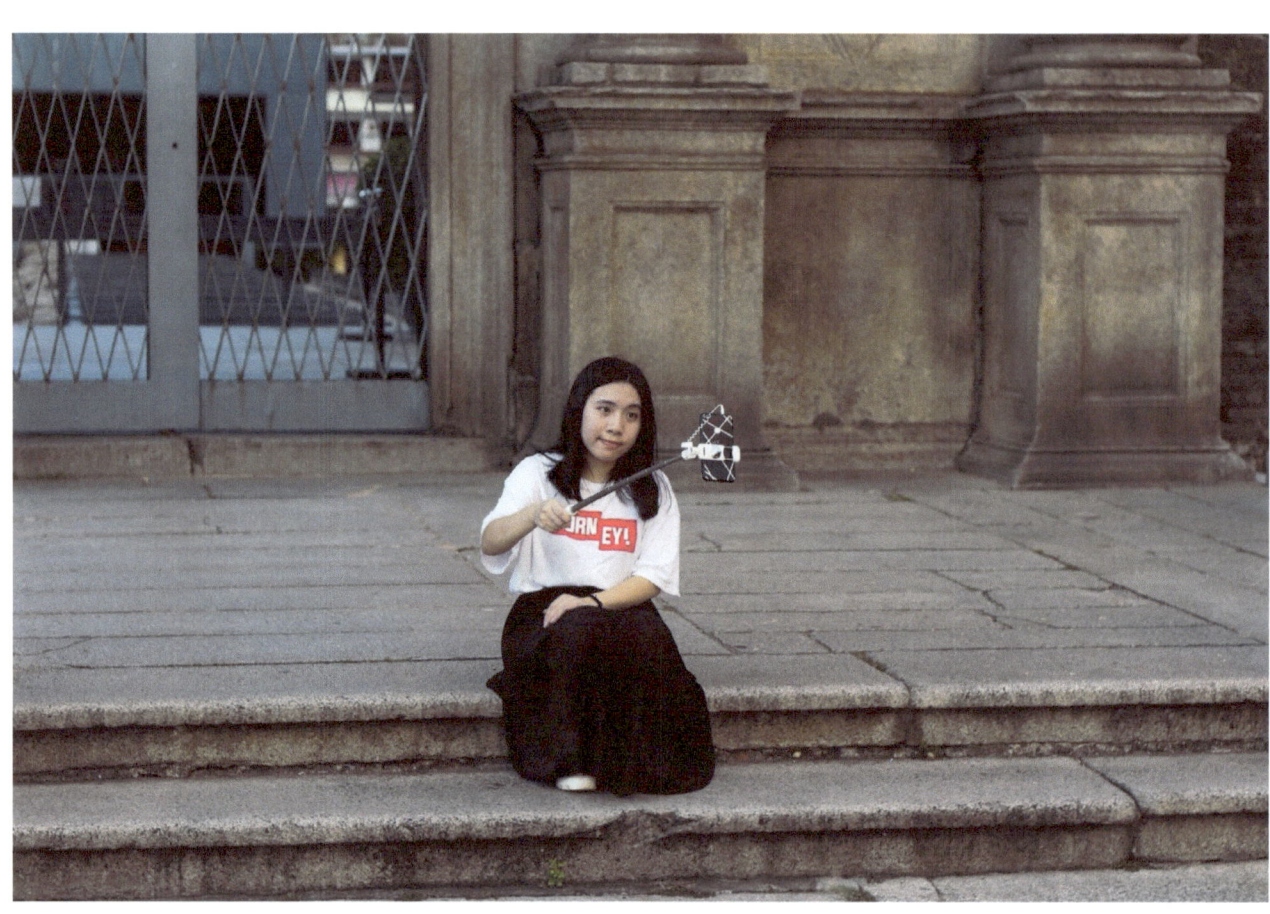

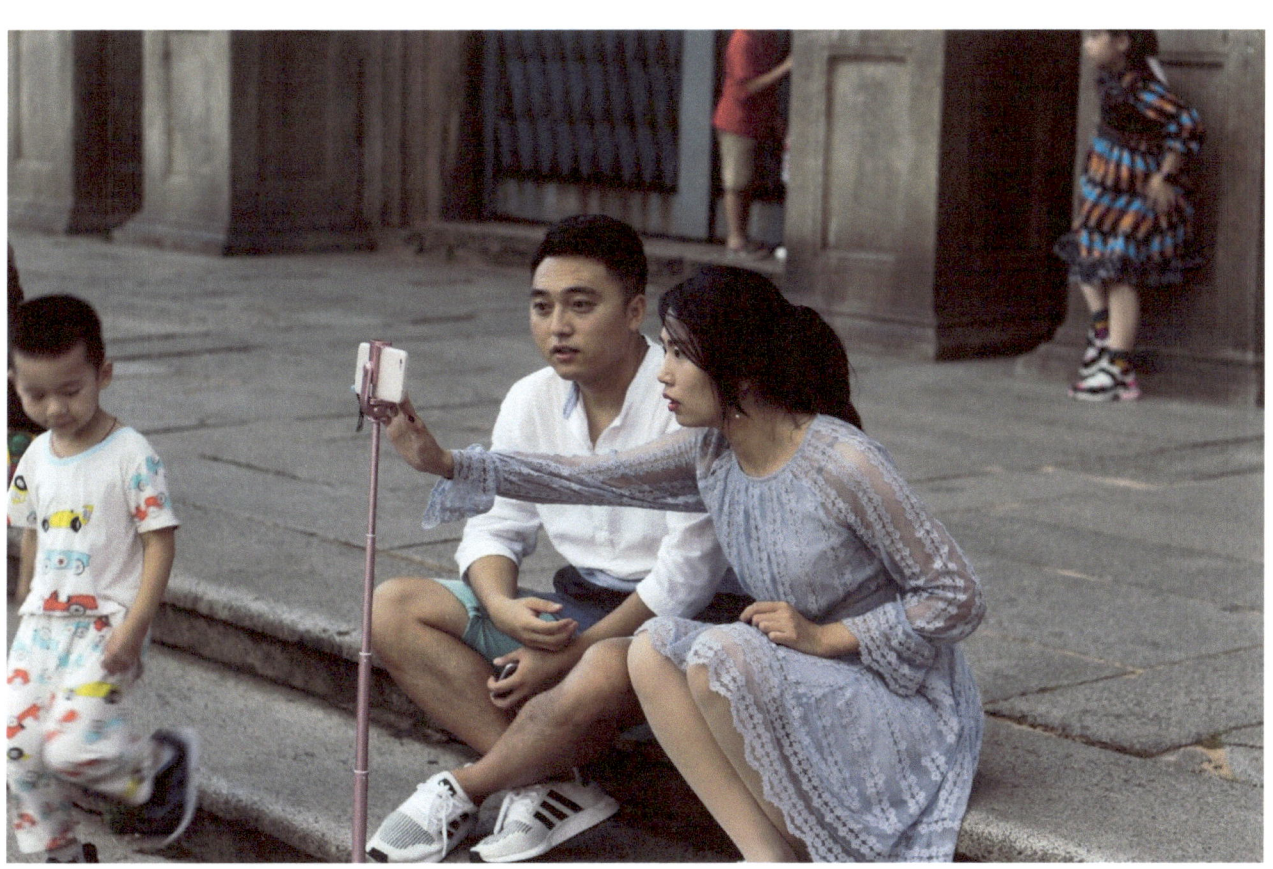

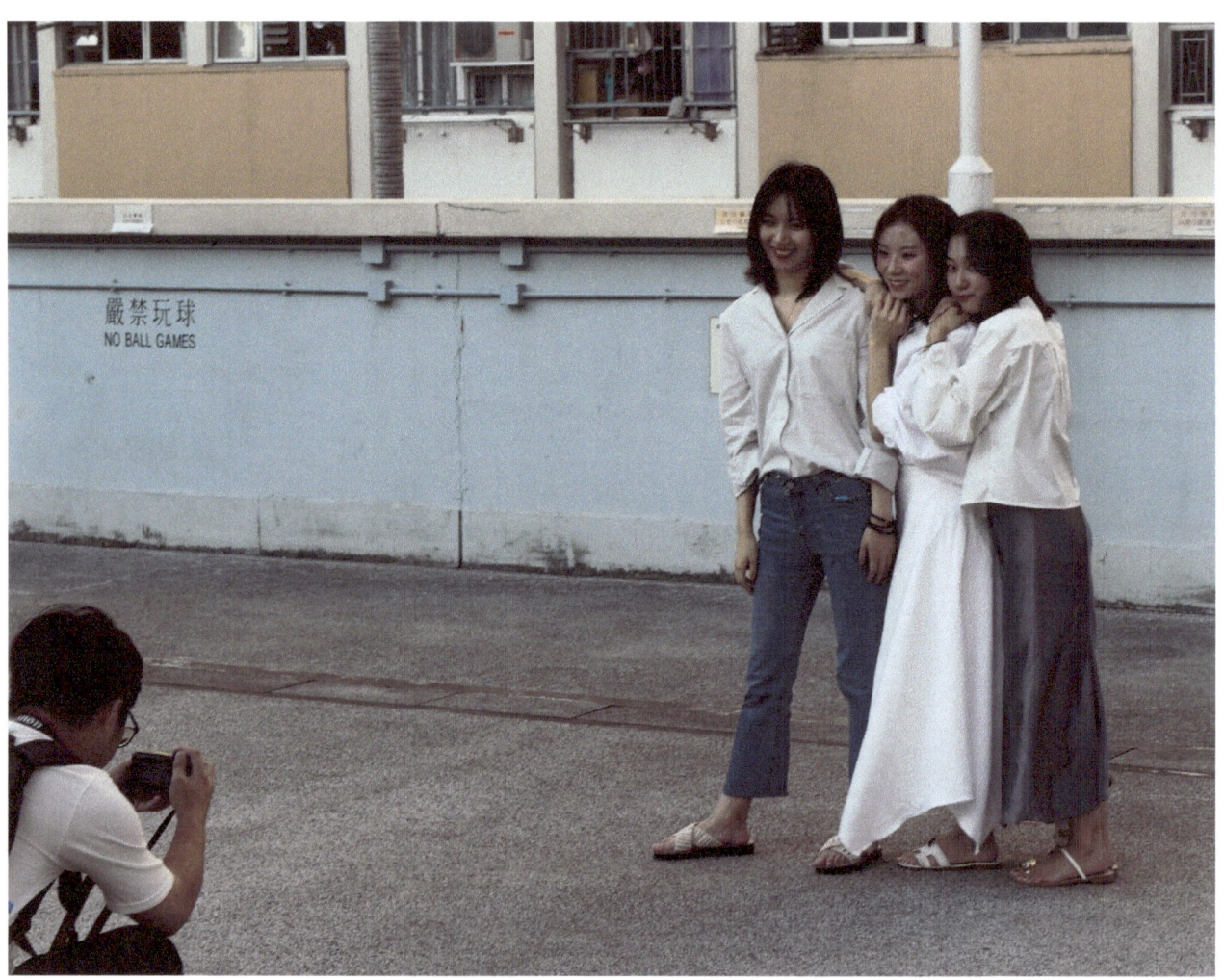

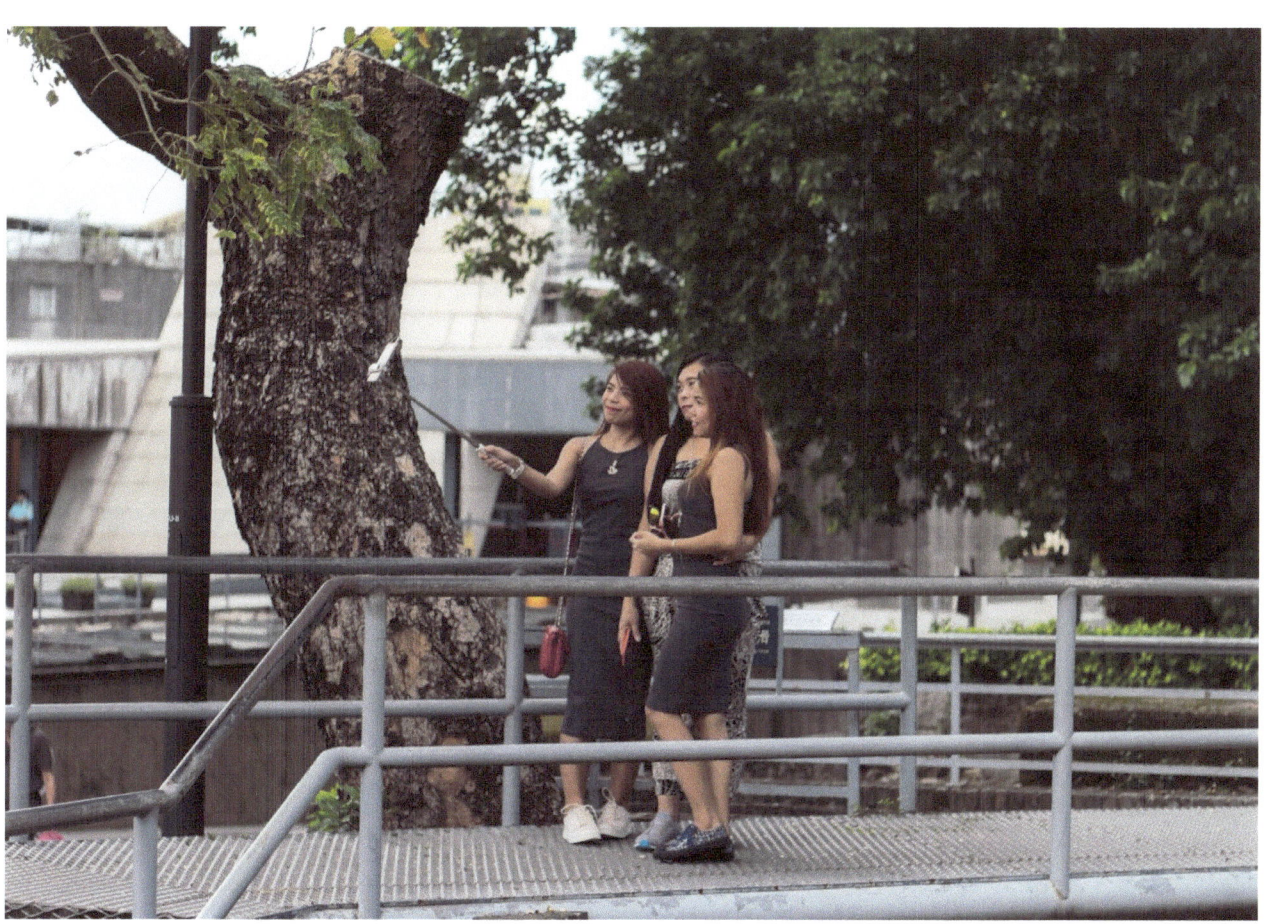

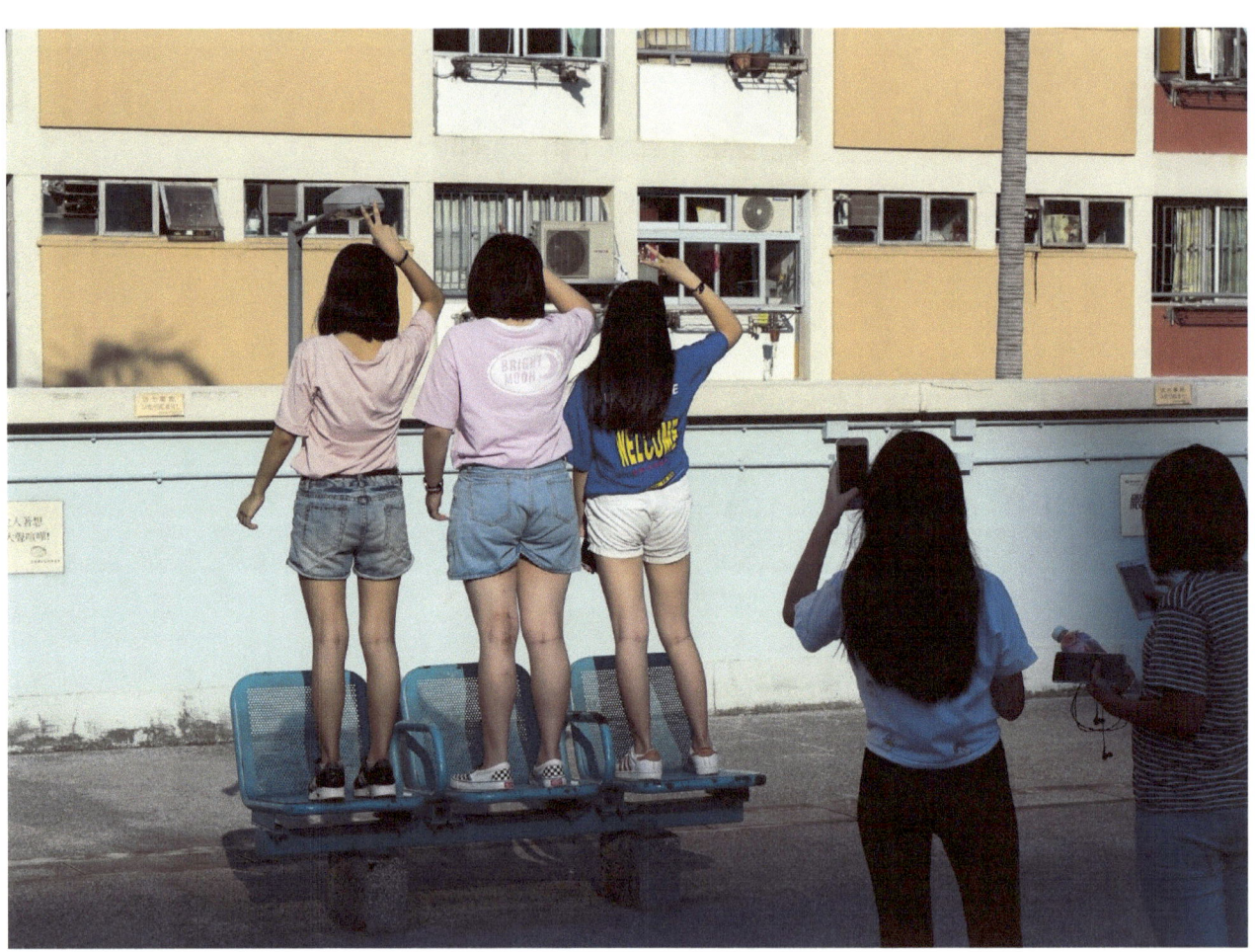

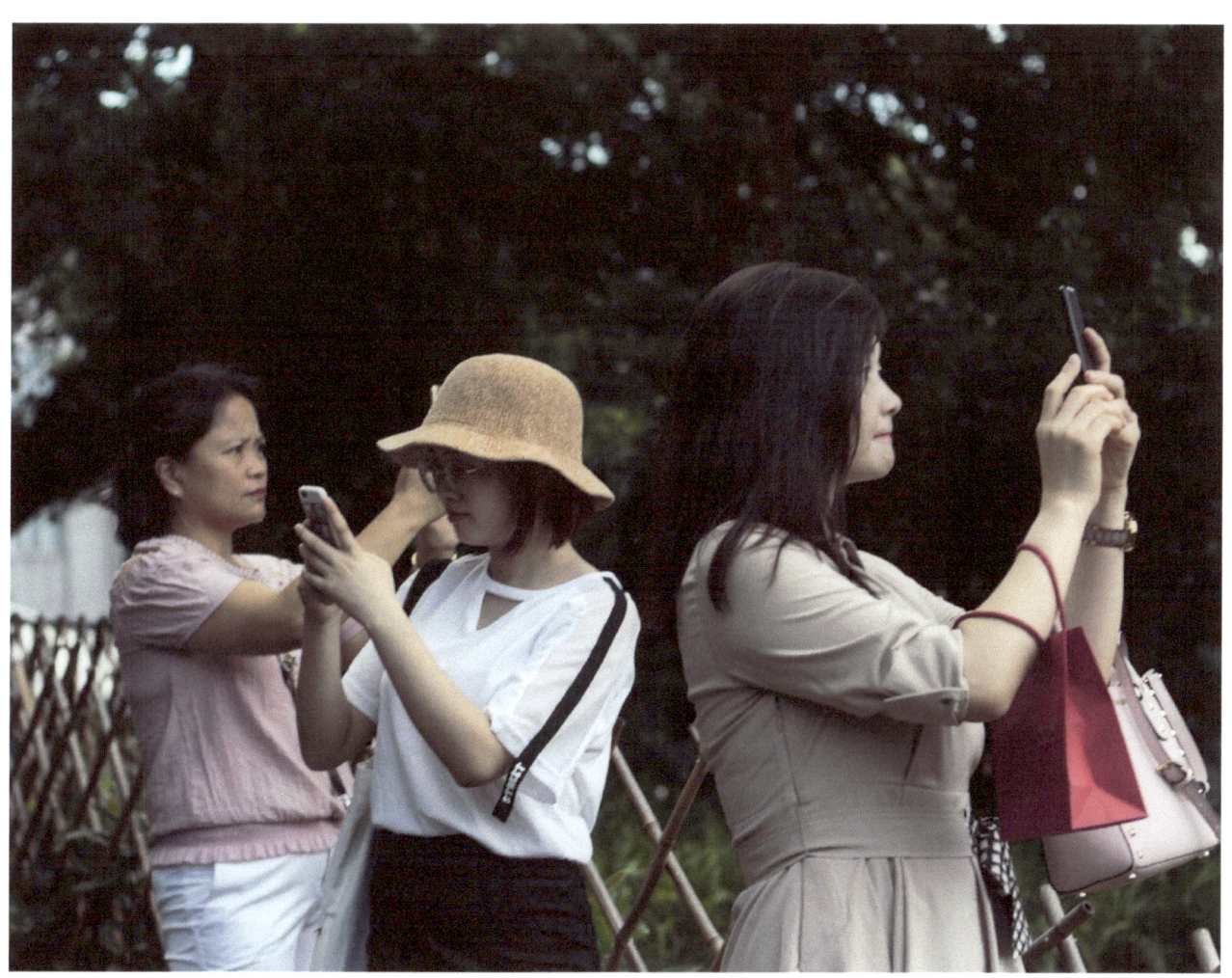

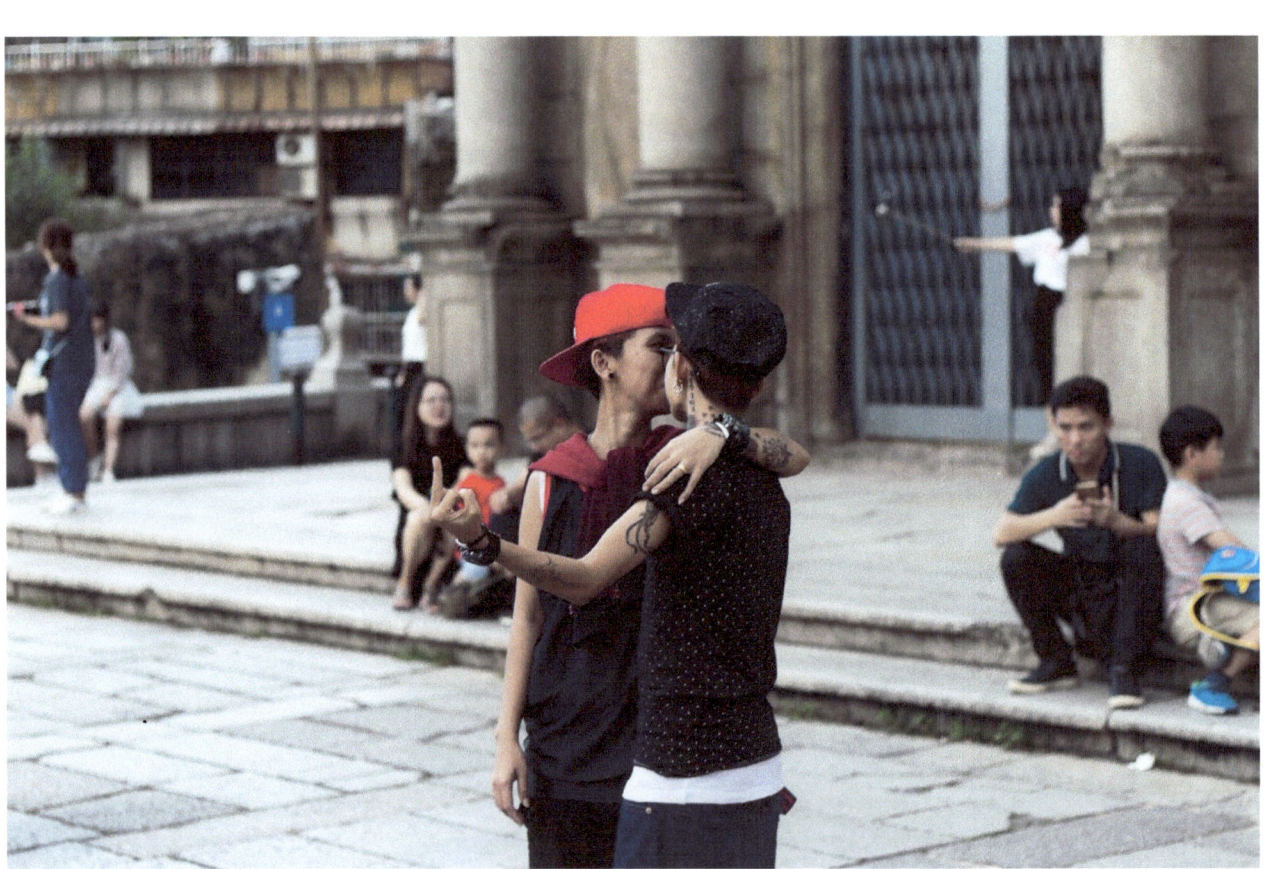

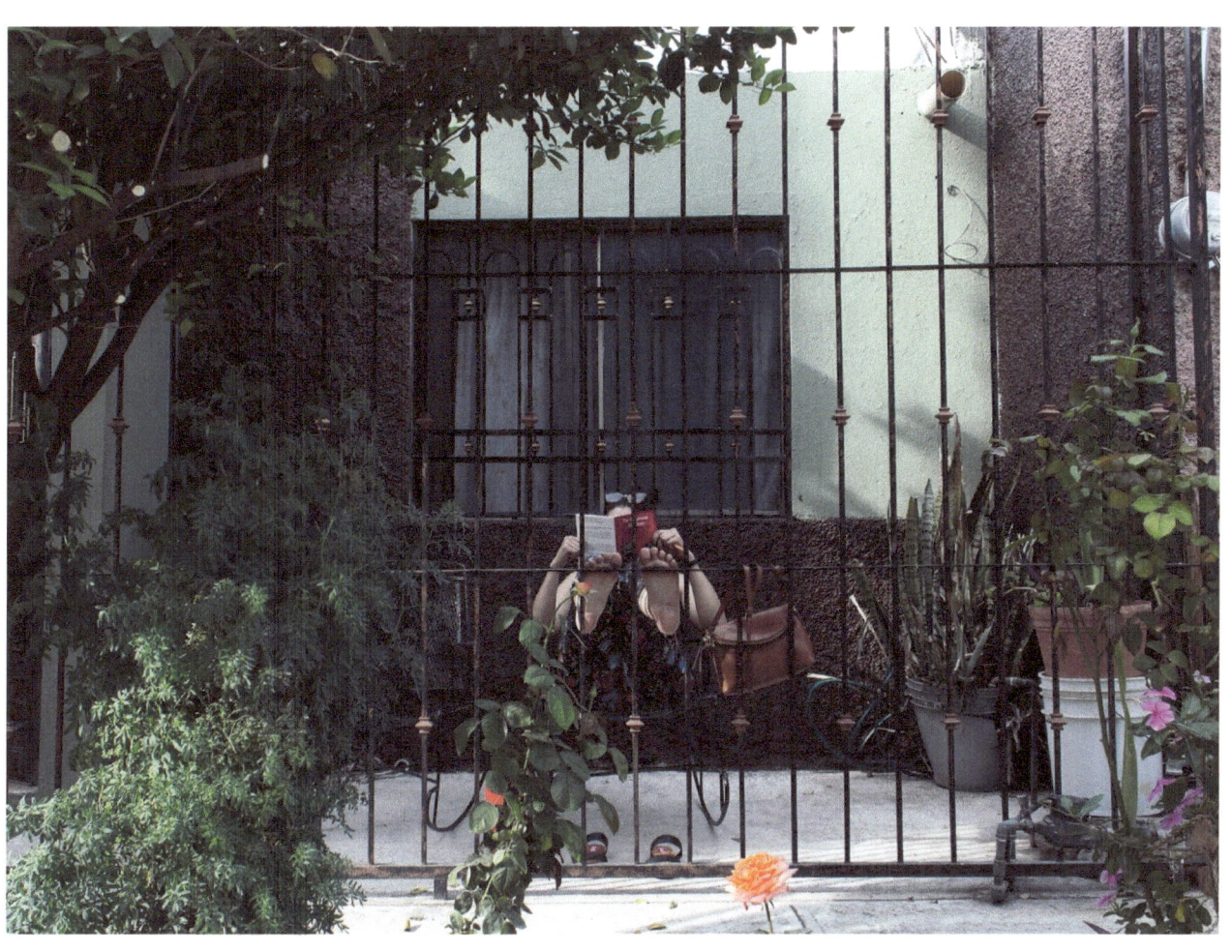

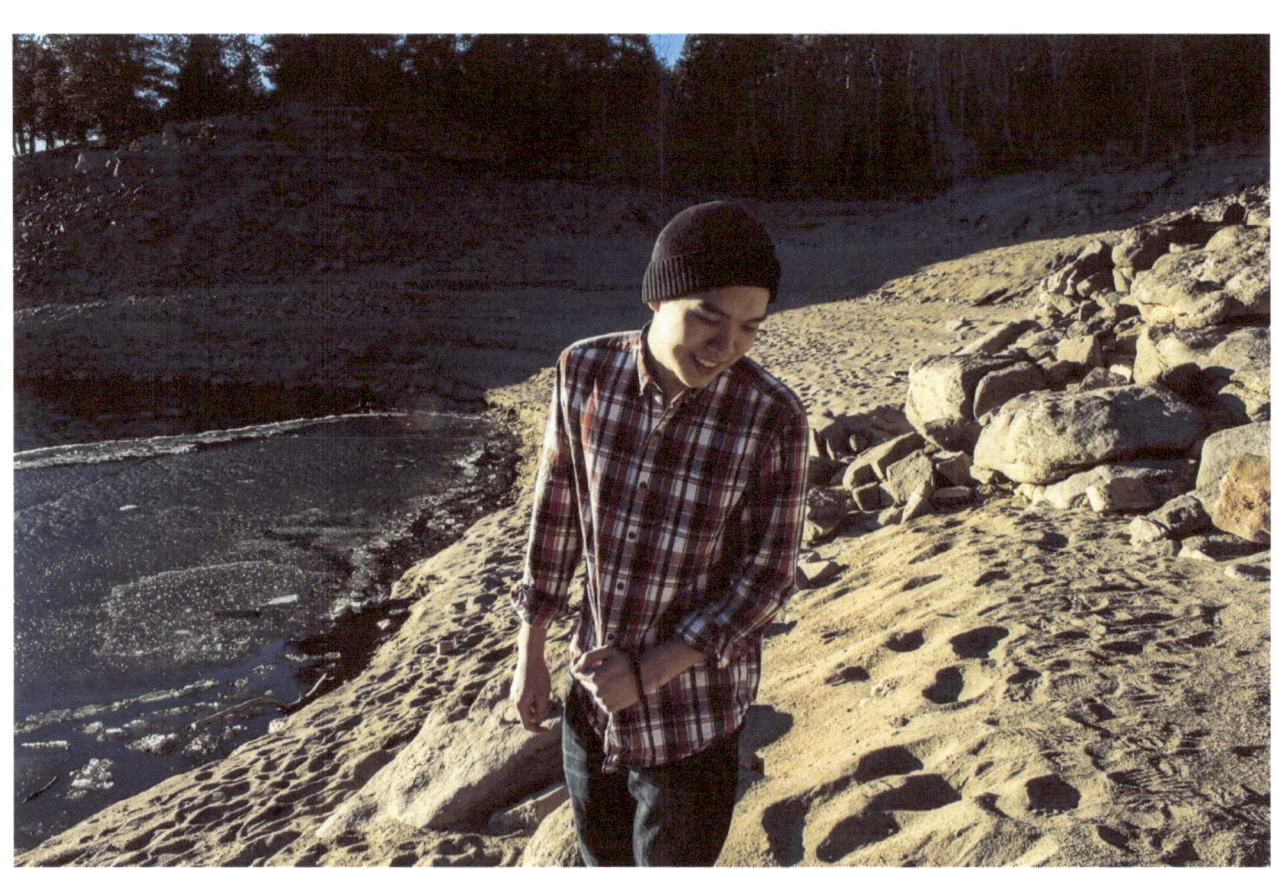

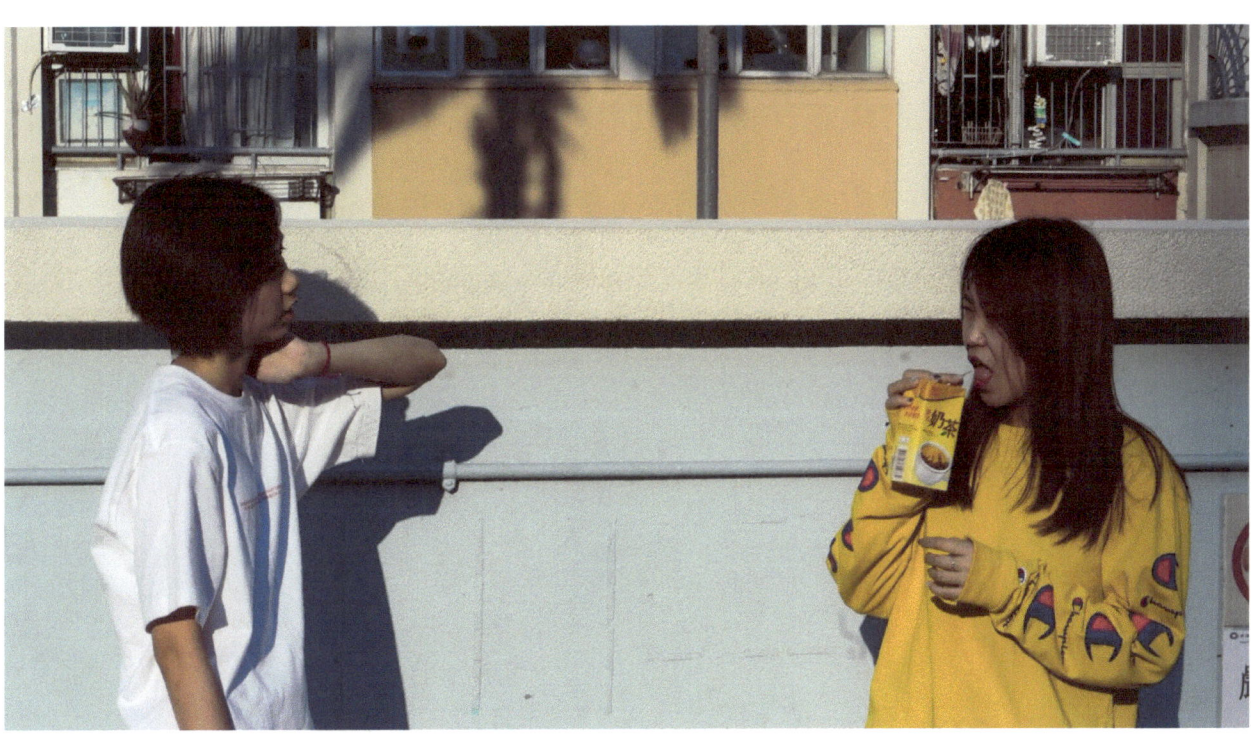

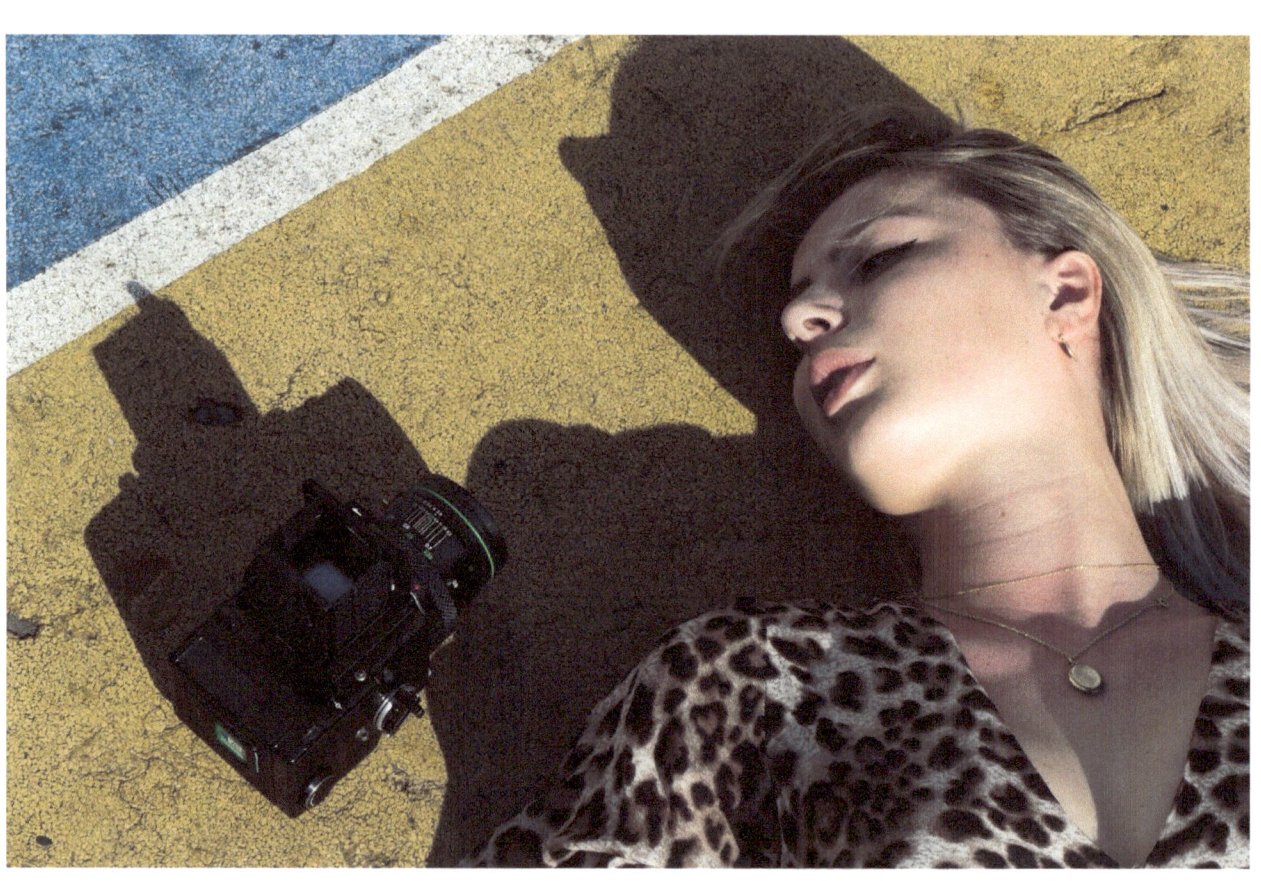

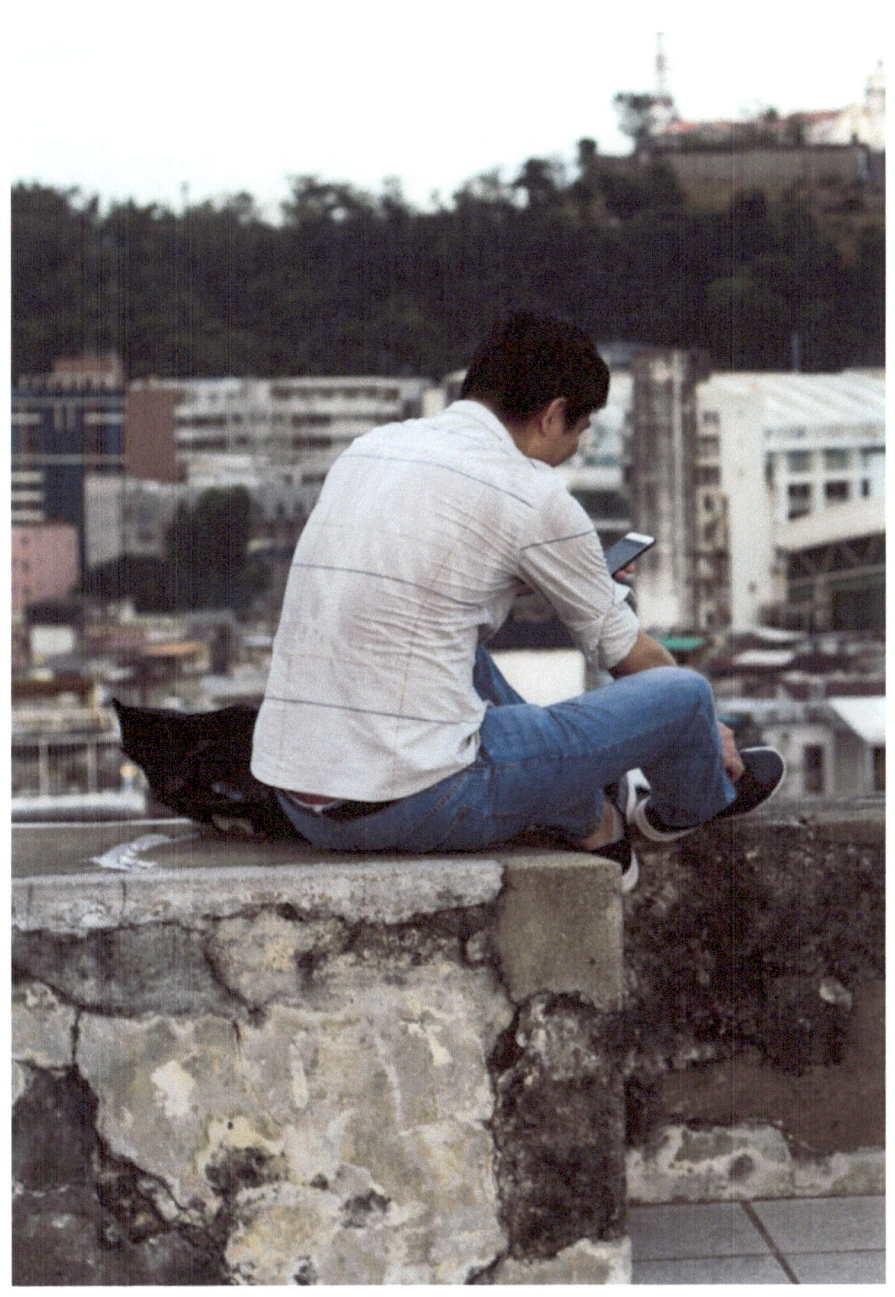

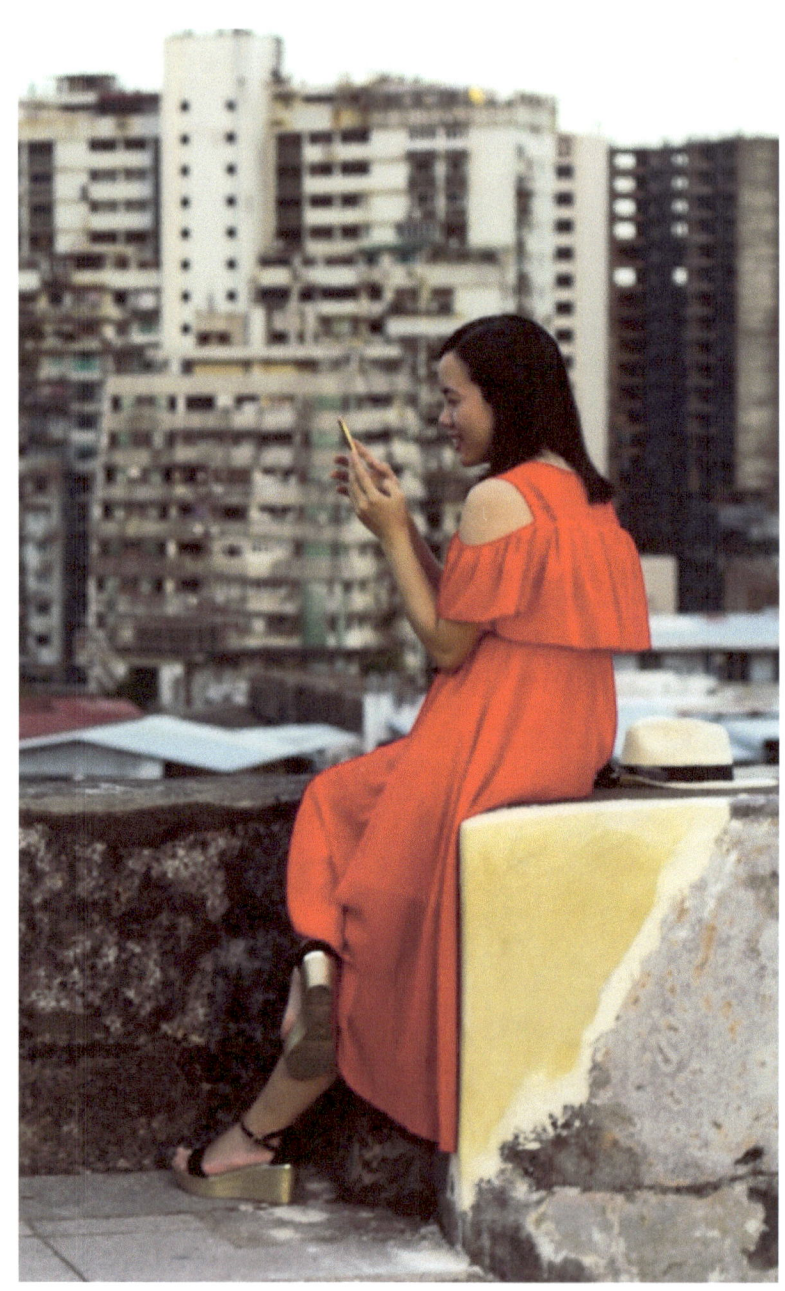

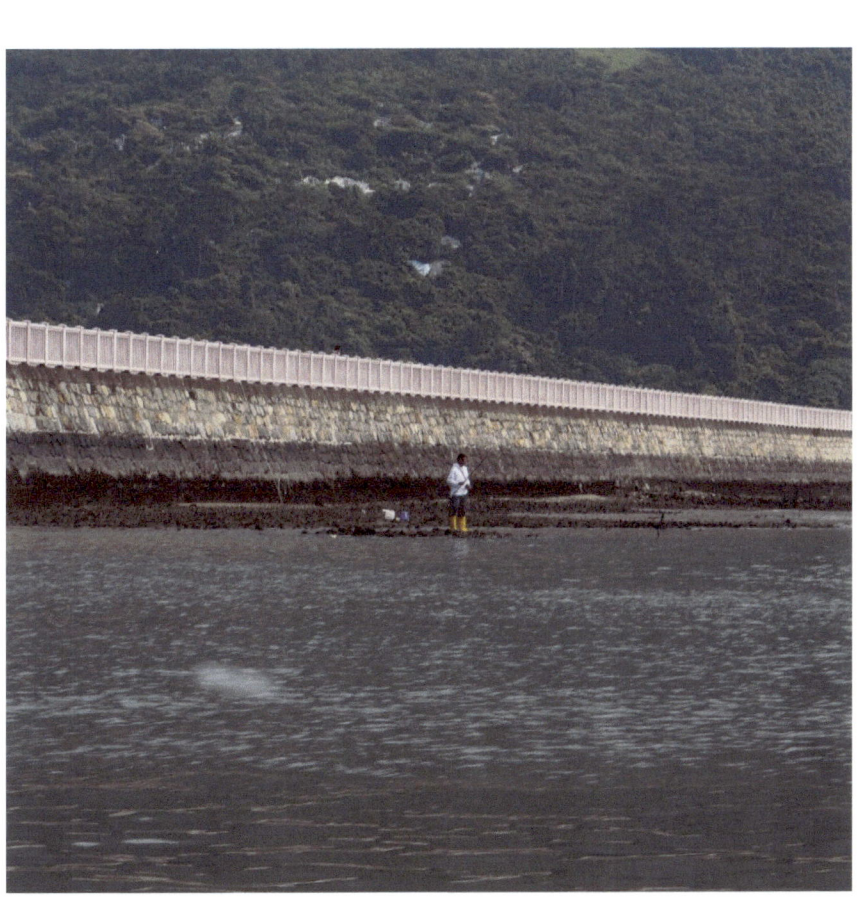

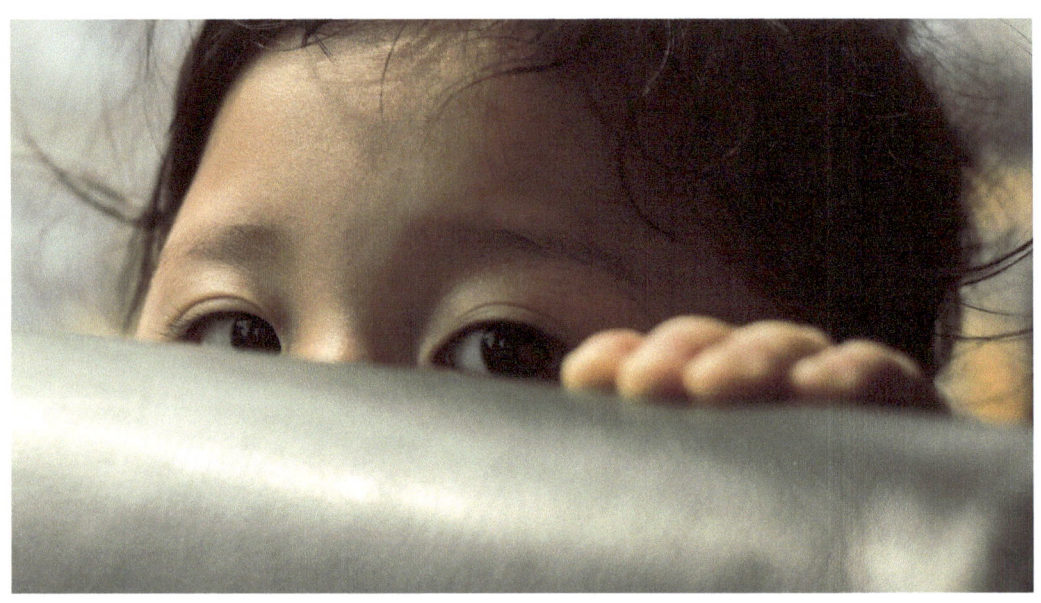

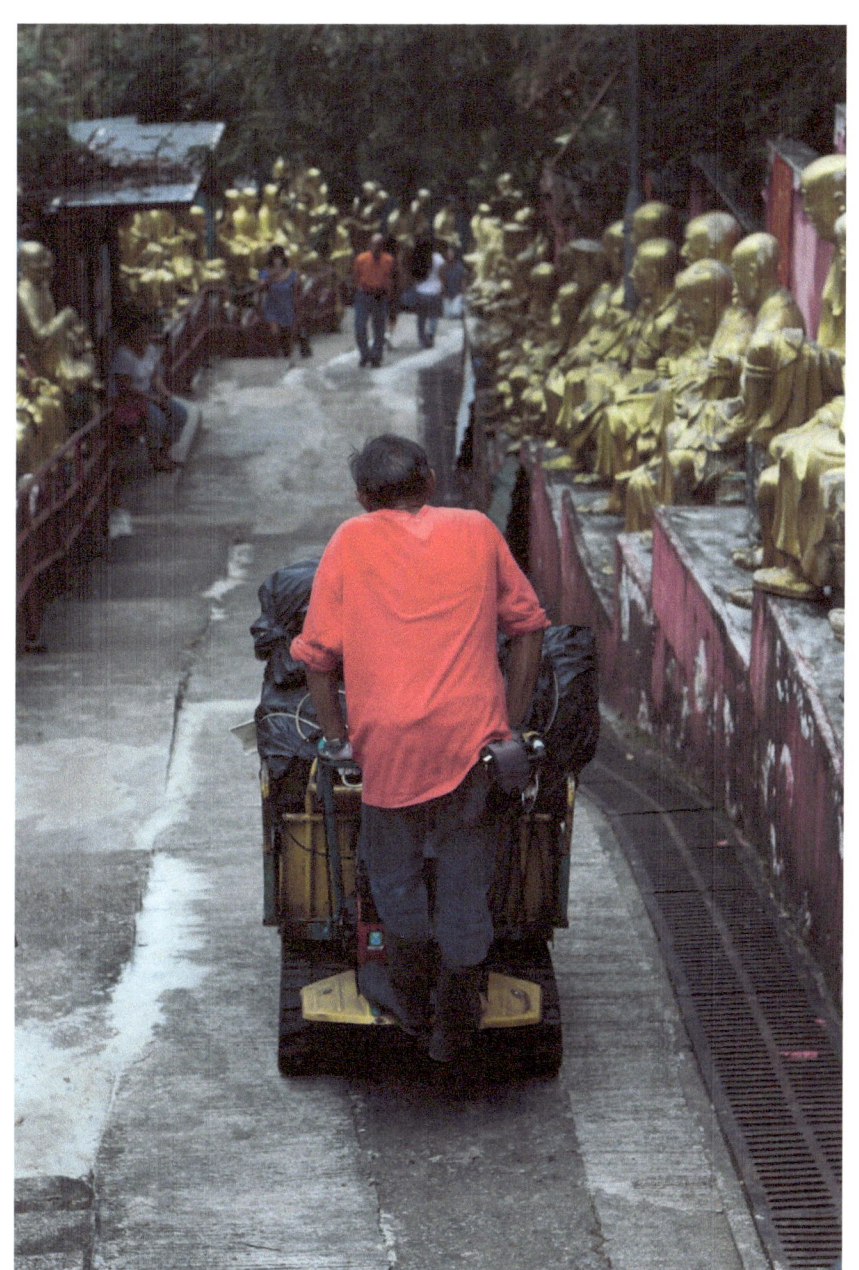

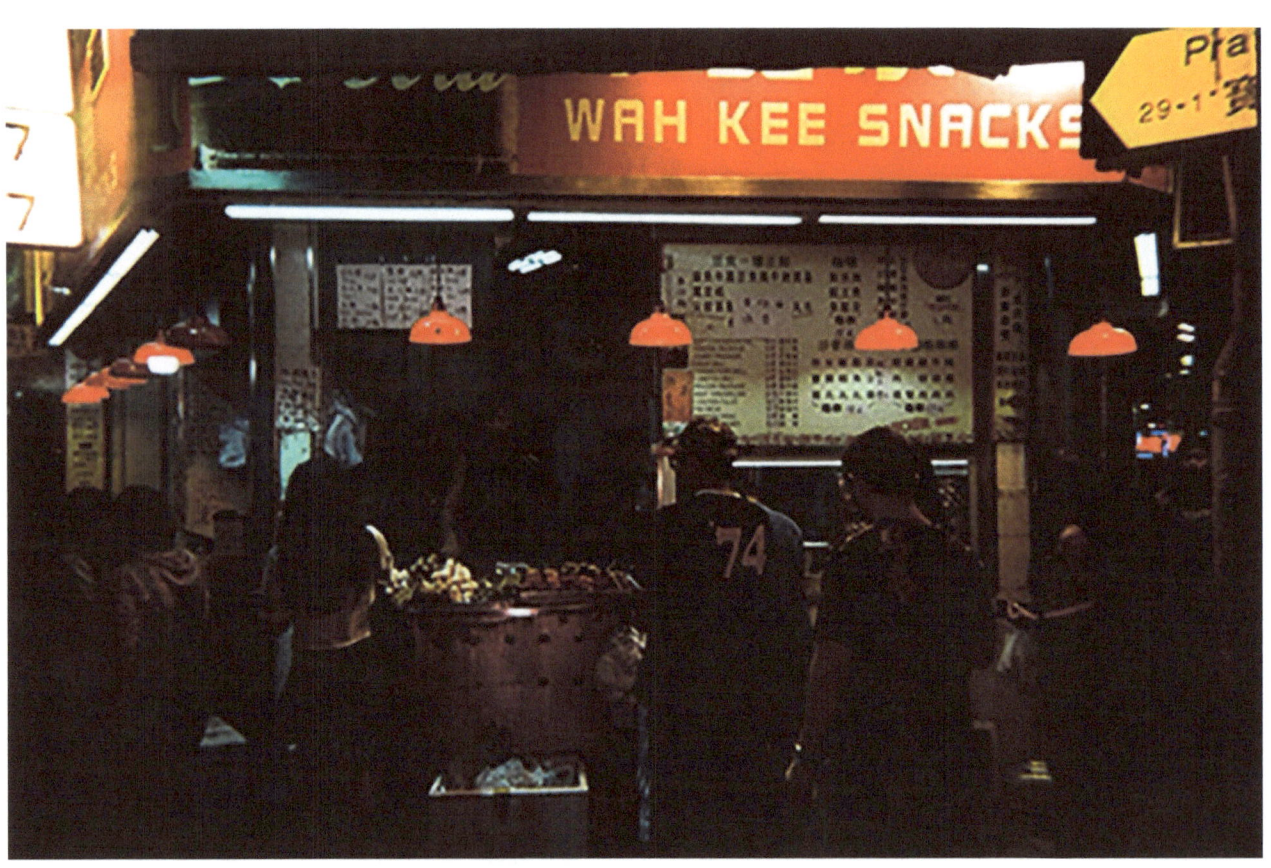

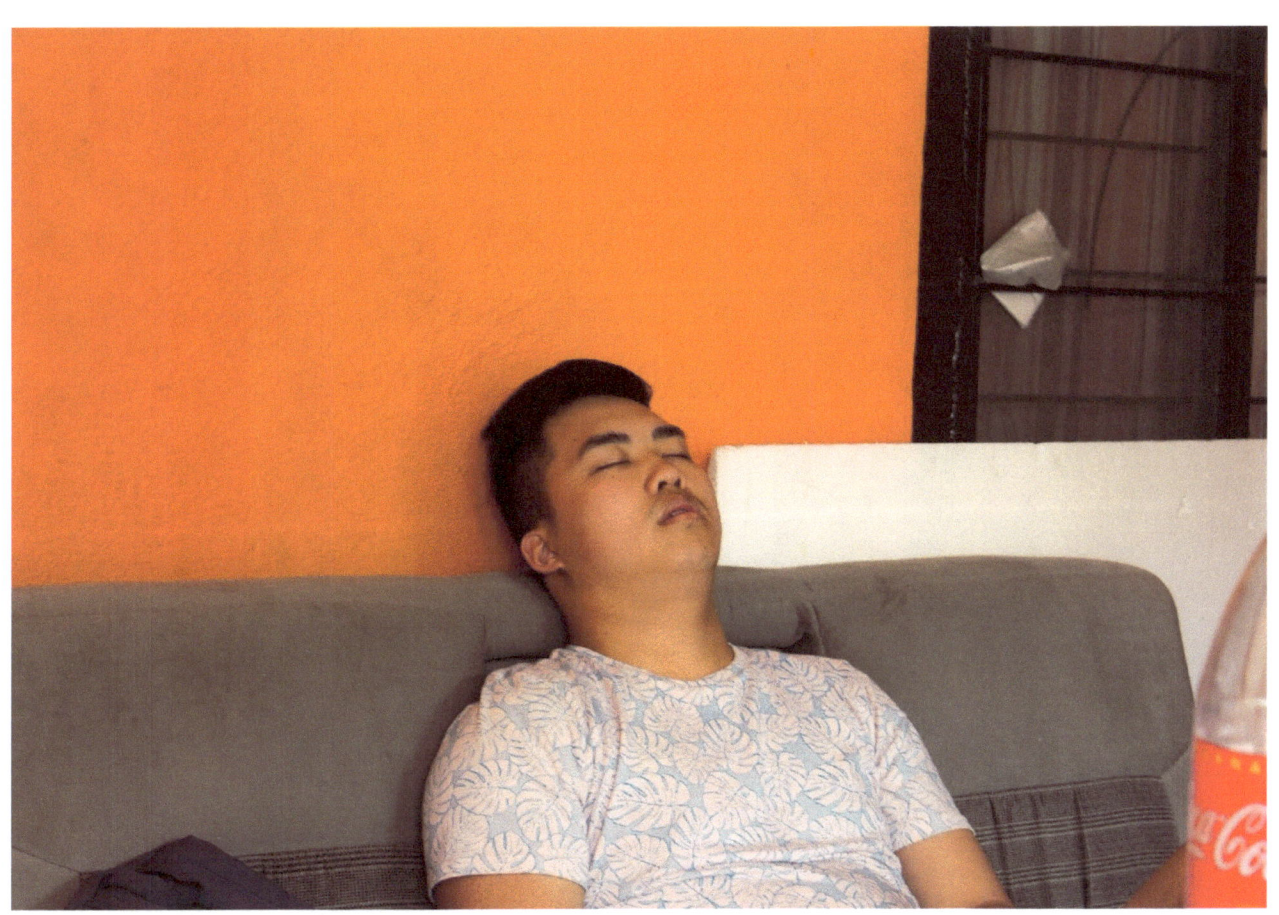

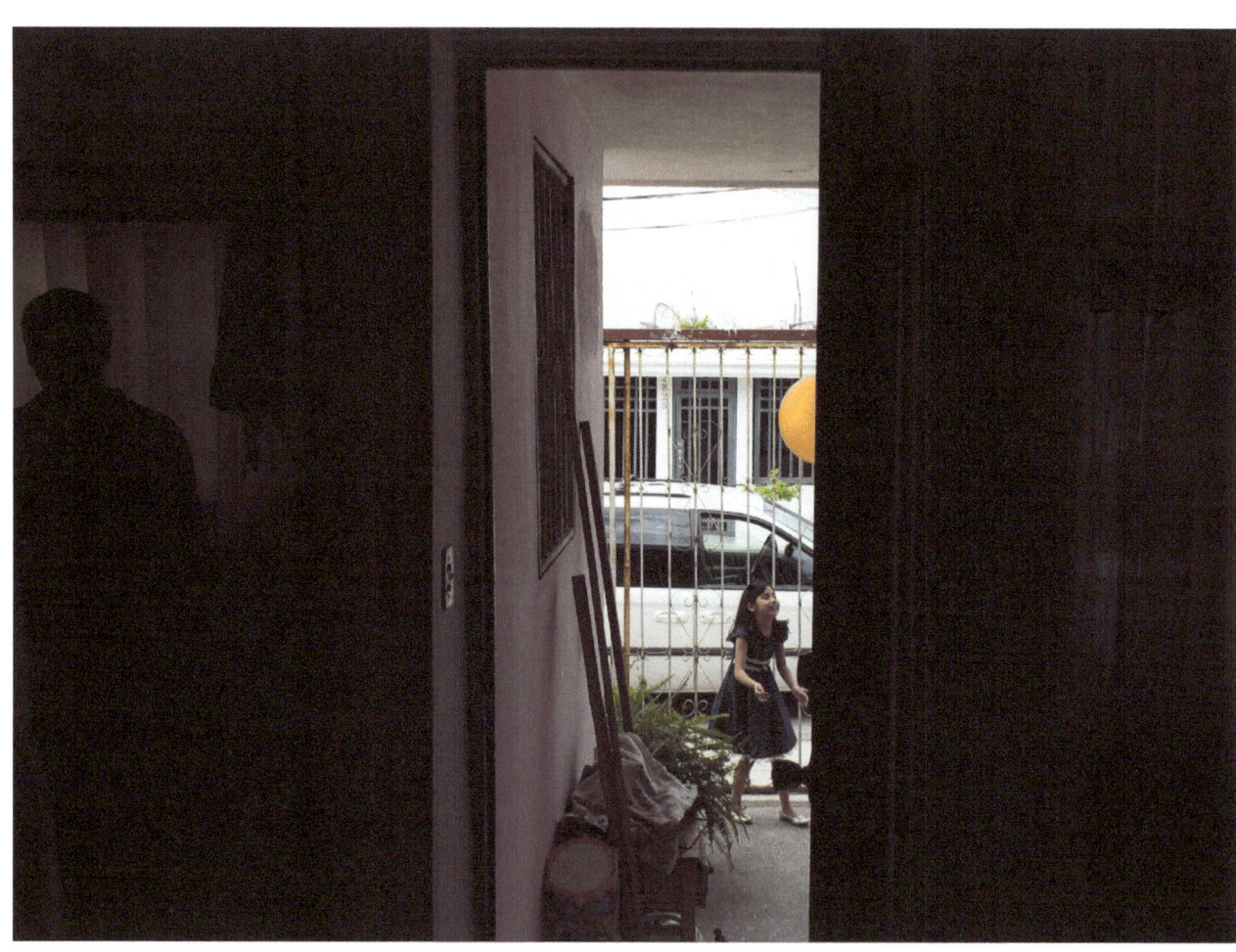

Most of these photos were taken using my Canon 1200D, equipped with a 50mm f/1.8mm.

The 3rd last photo was taken with a disposable Lomography 400 camera.

These photos were taken in various places around Mexico, the US and Hong Kong.

keiden.